Clovernook

CLOVERNOOK HOME FOR THE BLIND

Clovernook
HOME FOR THE BLIND

FOUNDED BY
GEORGIA AND FLORENCE TRADER
MAY 8, 1903

COMMONWEALTH BOOK COMPANY
St. Martin, Ohio

Copyright © and privately printed in 1957
Copyright © 2024 by Commonwealth Book Company, Inc.

All rights reserved. No part of this book may be reproduced in any form or by any means without the prior written consent of the publisher, excepting brief quotes used in reviews. Printed in the United States of America.

ISBN: 978-1-948986-62-5

THE STORY OF
THE TRADER SISTERS

By

LIBBY LACKMAN ACKLAND

TABLE OF CONTENTS

		Page
Chapter I	The Traders	11
Chapter II	The Crusade Begins	15
Chapter III	Clovernook	22
Chapter IV	A True Heroine	28
Chapter V	Clovernook's Friends	31
Chapter VI	Life On Tiptoes	36
Chapter VII	Two Angels	42
Chapter VIII	A Path of Roses	44
Chapter IX	The Dearest Place On Earth	49

I

THE TRADERS

*"Did God Give You
A Finer Harp To Play Upon
Because One String Was Missing?"**

These poignant lines were written, in grief and awe, shortly after the death March 12, 1944 of Georgia Duckworth Trader. The poet was a friend of the blind woman who gave vision to so many. But friend and stranger alike were moved to write myriad words about this sightless saint, who turned her handicap into opportunities for others. Gathered together, the words form a little chapter of their own in the history of mankind's gifts to mankind.

* * *

Mrs. Trader glanced out the window one day, and then leaned out in dismay.

"Florence," she called in genteel, strained horror, "what are you and Georgie doing?"

Across the street, in a muddy yard, a new house was rising. Climbing along its bare joists were two happy, carefree girls, engaged in a sport dear to the hearts of all normal youngsters. But one of the girls was blind.

It was a warm, lazy summer afternoon in Cincinnati, Ohio, about the year 1888. Mrs. Trader was engaged in housewifely pursuits common to women of comfortable, well-bred stations. Soon James would arrive home from

*Mona Downs

his insurance office and their eldest daughter, Effie, would drag herself away from her sketching, looking for supper. Happy little Louise, the youngest of their four daughters, was singing and playing in a nearby room.

Suddenly, Mrs. Trader sat down and began to laugh in her familiar, merry manner. It was terrible, she thought, in so many ways, but it was wonderful, too. Fate in its course had blinded Georgia, but God had given Georgia so much more. And God had given them all Florence.

She allowed herself to look back to the day when they had realized that their second daughter had imperfect eyesight. Living in Xenia, Ohio, at the time, they had taken the child to Cincinnati for help. Georgia, meanwhile, found her way around, learned to read and write, and accepted her parents' concern with little concern for herself.

When the child was 11, Mr. Trader sold his small oil well in Yellow Springs, Ohio, and moved his family to Cincinnati. There, they could be nearer eye specialists and Mrs. Trader's beloved brother, George Duckworth, for whom Georgia had been named. An operation on the 11-year old had followed, infection had set in, and the child had completely lost her eyesight.

Later the blind girl, grown into woman, oft was heard to say that her affliction was "providential."

And providential it was!

It brought about establishment of the Cincinnati Library Society for the Blind, the first institution in the city to provide free books to the sightless.

It brought about the first classes for blind children in the Cincinnati public schools.

It brought about the first program of eye examinations in the schools, and the first sight conservation classes.

It brought about Clovernook, the first home for blind women in the State of Ohio.

And it inspired two selfless young women, hand in

hand, to supplement these pioneering projects by:

Seeking out the blind in their lonely homes;

Teaching them to read, write, and otherwise employ idle hands and minds in a path away from darkness;

Watching over all their interests through militant attention to legislation and employment for their benefit, and

Providing an impetus for similar undertakings throughout the United States and the world.

Said Helen Keller, the internationally known spokesman for all the physically afflicted, many years later:

"Your sacrifices since the early days, when the world of the blind was still a mostly unchartered wilderness, cannot be enumerated."

When the Trader family moved from Xenia to Cincinnati, they established themselves in a large frame house, typical of the era, at 538 Hale Avenue, in the suburb of Avondale. The year was 1887. Family records show that Effie had been born in 1874, Georgia in 1876, Florence in 1878 and Louise in 1885, all in Xenia.

An acquaintance of those early days recalls the family as a happy one. Elizabeth Jane, the mother, who was known as Lizzie, was a pretty woman, always with a smile on her face. The father was tall, and fine looking. People always noticed the girls, because they were so prettily dressed, in frocks made by their mother and their grandmother Duckworth.

Shortly after Georgia's unsuccessful operation, her mother took her to Columbus to enter her in the State School for the Blind. At that time, there was no other place in the Middle West for a blind person to learn to read and write. A few days later, Mrs. Trader brought Georgia back with her. Her mother's heart could not bear to leave the child at the school. Instead, the mother resolved, she would learn New York Point, the system then used for reading by the blind, and teach it to Georgia.

At home Florence, a sweet-natured girl who resembled her mother the most, was in the third grade in the Avondale Public School. A few days after the return from Columbus, she started off to school one morning, her arm tucked in Georgia's.

That arm was to guide the blind sister for the next 57 years.

II

THE CRUSADE BEGINS

*"Her battle was fought in the dark. Her enemies were ignorance, helplessness, isolation and depression."**

When time came for the two girls to begin high school, they entered Miss Armstrong's private school. At Miss Armstrong's, the teachers would take Georgia into a private room at examination time. Contemporaries claim that she topped the class in her oral tests.

The blind girl had an amazing memory. When the family started playing cards, Mr. Trader decided that Georgie could participate, too. He took a deck of cards, and marked them with tiny indentations. Informal research since implies that this was the first instance of such markings.

As a woman, Georgia loved to play bridge, with a particular fondness for duplicate games. Her friends say that she felt she had an unfair advantage in the game.

"I feel as if I were cheating," she would often sigh, referring to the fact that she could remember the cards so easily.

As is true with so many of the blind, she could also play the piano well. "Mamma read the notes off to her. and she memorized them quickly," Florence recalls fondly.

It was in her junior year at Miss Armstrong's that Georgia became possessed with her first crusading desire

*Canon Gilbert Symons

to help other blind. Her after-school hours, for many years, had been enriched with the reading of books printed in the New York Point system. Each book had to come by express from Columbus, and cost the Trader family 50 cents apiece.

"What of those who do not have the 50 cents?" Georgia asked one day.

It was the year 1900 when the two girls' schooling was finished. Immediately both set off to call on N.D.C. Hodges, librarian of the Cincinnati Public Library, who was to support the girls strongly in their activities for many years to come. Consultations with other library officials soon brought this word back: The library would put the books on its shelves, if the Trader girls would raise the money to buy them.

Georgia and Florence set off blithely to raise the money. It was not so easy as they originally thought. But as the years went by they set off just as blithely, time and again, to raise many, many thousands of dollars.

About this time William A. Procter, president of the Procter and Gamble Company and son of one of its founders, came into the lives of the Trader girls. A great philanthropist, his interest in their work and their welfare looms large and importantly in the bit of history they were about to write.

Georgia and Mr. Procter put the first books on the library shelves, she with her own nucleus of volumes, he with the Bible and 50 copies of histories and lives of prominent men and women. The soap manufacturer sent to England for his donation. The 50 books were done in Moon Type, a system of embossed printing much easier for older people to read.

At the suggestion of the library officials, the girls had gathered statistics on the number of blind in the area, and found that there were 400 within their reach. Armed with this figure and an initial subscription of $500 for books, they promptly laid plans for creating an organization that could carry on their work.

In March, 1901, at a meeting at the Avondale Presbyterian Church, the Cincinnati Library Society for the Blind was founded. The Trader girls had quickly discovered that they had two special talents, which they proceeded to use all their lives in the interests of others. One was to raise money. The other was to enlist volunteers to help them with their work.

Not long after activities started at the library, they had prominent men and women down there, reading to the blind and putting on entertainments for them. Murray Seasongood, one of Cincinnati's mayors, who had been a schoolmate of the girls, read Shakespeare aloud for years. The well known writer, John Uri Lloyd, loved to stage little entertainment programs.

Early in the game, the Traders realized that they could put the books on the shelves, but little could come of the effort without an aggressive program. Their aggressiveness was initiated in two ways. They obtained street car passes from local transit companies for the blind and their guides. And they sought out the sick, lonely and indigent in their own homes.

The Trader girls' invasion of the blind's enforced isolation began to mushroom. Georgia sent out word that she would be at the library to teach reading and writing, free of charge. Florence let it be known that she would teach games of cards, how to tell time, and how to thread needles. With the street car passes available, attendance doubled at the readings, which now included courses in English literature, French history and political science.

A scant two years later, in January, 1903, a report of the library society said:

"Since the teaching began in July, 1901, 48 have been

taught to read, two to read music, 24 given instruction in writing, and 20 taught to thread needles."

A bill passed by Congress in 1905 was instrumental in the Trader girls spreading their wings even farther. The bill allowed all books in embossed type, not weighing more than 10 pounds, to be sent through the mails free. Soon large, heavy volumes were being mailed by the library society to sightless persons all over the country.

The girls' instructions in sewing, knitting and crocheting, in which Florence took a leading role, received a terrific added momentum in 1912. The Ohio Commission for the Blind appropriated $58,000 to furnish material for blind workers.

The commission was to pay the workers for their labor, and soon Georgia and Florence had blind women earning as much as $3.60 a week. Crash toweling, materials and yarn were handed out to be made into towels, wash cloths, night slippers, baby sacks, shawls and aprons. The blind women would bring their completed work to the library once a week, get paid for it, and receive more material.

Meanwhile the Trader girls had not forgotten blind children. By 1903 Georgia had started a class for kindergartners at the library, with the aid of volunteers. Older children also were being taught reading, writing, arithmetic and geography, and handiwork within the capabilities of their small fingers. These were children whose parents did not want to send them away to the state school, in Columbus.

Realizing that the young minds of sightless youngsters needed far more time devoted to their education than they could allot, the girls began to make repeated representations to the Cincinnati School Board. At long last, in September, 1905, a department for the blind was opened in a building with a school for the deaf.

It was the second school for the blind in connection

BLIND CHILDREN ALIGHT FROM THEIR SCHOOL BUS (CIRCA 1905)

CLASS IN BRAILLE HELD AT PUBLIC LIBRARY
IN THE FOREGROUND IS A DEAF-BLIND GIRL READING THE LIPS OF HER GRANDMOTHER.

THE CARY COTTAGE

WM. A. PROCTER WITH GEORGIA TRADER, LEFT, AND FLORENCE TRADER

with a public school system in the United States, its predecessor being in Chicago. In 1909, the Trader girls persuaded the School Board to allow the blind children to go into classes with the seeing. This practice is still continued.

On the morning that school opened in 1905, only four blind youngsters turned up for classes. Investigation by the Traders revealed that parents were unable to leave their work to bring any others.

So another campaign was launched. While two local funeral directors, Messrs. Busse and Borgmann, temporarily conveyed the children to school, Cincinnati's Commercial Tribune, at the instigation of the Traders, sponsored a drive for $600. The money was to finance a bus, team of horses and driver for one year. School children's pennies and nickels helped to oversubscribe the fund. Later the School Board took over the transportation.

Within a short time, Georgia and Florence introduced two other projects that are sometimes lost in the wave of later undertakings. In cooperation with a Cincinnati physician, Dr. Frank D. Phinney, who gave his services, examinations of eyes were begun in the public schools. Seeing the importance of this precaution, the School Board soon made this part of their program. On the heels of this, Trader persuasiveness caused the same board to open a department in the schools for the conservation of sight.

III

CLOVERNOOK

"One sweetly solemn thought
Comes to me o'er and o'er
I'm nearer home today, today
Than I have been before."

Sweet words these are, from the familiar hymn by poetess Phoeby Cary, and they spell Clovernook. The birthplace of the famous Cary sisters, Cincinnati-born poetesses, Clovernook was to influence all their writings, during the long years after they left it. For more than 50 years now, it has been the home of countless blind women, made possible by the Trader sisters.

Local historians, since the turn of the century, have gloried in trying to meld the lives of the two pairs of Cincinnati sisters.

"Which was the finer gift of Clovernook—the Cary sisters gift of beauty or the Trader sisters gift of light?" was the dramatic editorial penned in 1927.

The Carys—Alice, the older, and Phoebe—were two Ohio farm girls who, in 1850, invaded New York and quickly captured the big city's literary heart. Devoted to one another, they worked together, studied together, wrote and died together. Their bond was a deep love of nature, a hunger for knowledge, a genius for poetry and a consuming passion for goodness and beauty.

Clovernook had been built in 1832 by their father,

Robert Cary. The bricks were baked on the place. How many changes were made in subsequent years is difficult to surmise, but the basic architecture has been preserved.

The front of the two-story house, facing on what is best known as Hamilton Pike, is lighted by five windows, with three large slabs of stone leading to the entrance. The east side is the focal point. There, an overhanging balcony, supported by unique round brick pillars, shades a terrace. The terrace was originally made of flagstones which had been taken from a nearby creek, numbered, and laid exactly as in the creek bed. An old well, with its oaken bucket, stands at the edge of the terrace.

Inside the 19th Century cottage is what is known as the "manuscript cupboard." It is a little opening, under a front stairway, where the poet sisters hid their writings from a disapproving stepmother.

In the year 1903, Georgia and Florence Trader saw in a local newspaper that the historic home of the famous Cary sisters was for sale.

Its owner was a Mrs. M. Louise Thomas, described as a wealthy and prominent woman from New York, who had purchased the property in 1895, with the hope of keeping it "in the family." During their girlhood, Mrs. Thomas and the Carys had known each other through their church affiliation. Later, in New York, that friendship had continued.

Mrs. Thomas' hope had been that Clovernook would be purchased and turned into a park or some kind of memorial to the sweet associations surrounding it. Finding no such philanthropist to sustain her sentiments, she finally put the place on the market for $10,000.

The day after reading of this, Georgia and Florence took a streetcar out to the place, situated in the Cincinnati suburb of Mt. Healthy. It was a beautiful ride, with the sweet air of open country sweeping through their car.

Miles of fertile ground, with sleepy farm houses and busy farms, spread away to the horizon on either side.

Arriving at the Cary place, they found 26 acres, divided into 15 acres of clover; three of pasture; three of wood lot, mostly sugar beech; three of garden, and two surrounding the dwelling, consisting chiefly of a fine grove of sugar maples, blackberries and flowers. In addition there were two 30-foot wells, of the purest drinking water; three springs; about 100 fruit trees, and long stretches of grapevine. The eight-room brick house stood 100 feet back from the turnpike.

As Georgia wrote later, the girls "were quite pleased with the location."

"While the house was small, we felt it was large enough to start with, and there was ground enough on which to build later if we could."

What the girls wanted to start was a home for blind women. In all their work among the sightless, they had been distressed by one shocking fact: the homeless blind had only infirmaries to go to, where they were shut off from books and other occupations designed for them. At first the Traders had sought to have a home built with government funds; letters had gone off to both state and national officials. One batch of the correspondence preserved by Florence shows a disinterested response from Ohio's governor. It also reveals that Georgia and Florence had made a trip to Columbus to call on the good man, only to find that he was unavailable.

After viewing Clovernook and being "pleased" with it, Georgia and Florence sped to the office of their good friend and benefactor, William A. Procter. Would he advise them on how to raise the money to purchase the place?

The great philanthropist was used to receiving calls from the girls. In fact, he looked forward to them on a weekly basis, only requesting that they set a definite time, and be prompt. Mr. Procter adored them both, and fretted over Georgia like a mother hen. In spite of Florence's devoted care of her sister, he apparently had a constant fear of blind Georgia's being struck down in her travels.

Mindful of the ever-increasing burdens which these two angels of the blind wanted to shoulder, he tried to curb their zeal. But at the same time he couldn't curb his indulgence of their wishes. They had talked to him before about starting a home for the blind, and he had asked them not to attempt such a gigantic project. But the afternoon they sought his advice about Clovernook, he grabbed the telephone and called his real estate agent.

"These little girls want that house. Get it for them," he said, and the next day, March 11, 1903, the purchase was completed.

Miss Florence loves to recall the consternation she and her family caused the agent before the sale. Bright and early the morning after Mr. Procter had promised to buy Clovernook, the two sisters and their mother, with their devoted minister, the Rev. Dr. Charles Frederick Goss, went out to see the place. Spotting them, the agent rushed them into the barn, and told them to hide there.

"He said the price would go up, if such intense interest were displayed."

The day after the purchase, Mr. Procter called on the girls' mother in distress. "I don't think I did the right thing at all," he told her.

But hundreds of Cincinnatians did. Stories of the purchase were splashed all over the newspapers, and subscriptions were sought for renovating, furnishing and maintaining the place. Soon vans of furniture and wagon loads of supplies were climbing the hill to Mt. Healthy. In addition to linens, carpeting, kitchen utensils and farm equipment, there were such donations as a cow, a barrel of salt, and the paper, and work of papering, five of the rooms.

In a pattern which they followed from there on, the Misses Trader invited the public, great and humble alike, to the formal dedication of Clovernook on May 8, 1903.

Both Georgia and Florence were exquisite looking girls. A reporter of the period described the "lovely picture" they presented, as they stood in the low-ceilinged parlor of the Cary cottage, and received the hundreds who had come to appraise and applaud. Dressed in "the purest of white dainty lace gowns," the girls were still aglow with the emotion that had accompanied a simple and, to them, sacred ceremony a few hours earlier. At noon that day, in the presence of the entire Trader family and a few very close friends, William A. Procter had turned over the deed to Clovernook, which was to be used perpetually as "a home for the worthy blind." He had made Georgia and Florence the sole trustees.

The hours of the opening reception were from 2 to 10 p.m., and all during this time crowded streetcars unloaded passengers in front of the place and prominent men and women drove up in carriages. At 4 p.m., in the shade of the lawn, the dedication ceremony took place. The speakers were Dr. Goss and the Rev. Paul Matthews, a son-in-law of Mr. Procter. Like the countless benefit fetes, which followed at Clovernook each anniversary date, the visitors were treated to a program of entertainment. An orchestra, placed on the balcony of the cottage, played at intervals throughout the afternoon and evening. Mr. and Mrs. Trader and the Misses Effie and Louise Trader were on hand to assist with the hospitalities, and so were a dozen other volunteers enlisted by Georgia and Florence. As in subsequent years, women associated with Cincinnati's most prominent families lent willing hands. Among other duties, they dispensed the "light refreshments." One news account of the day, noting that good old country buttermilk was on the menu, added that "delicious lemonade" was offered to "those city folk who fail to appreciate buttermilk."

In the midst of all this Georgia was quoted as having told a reporter for the Cincinnati Enquirer, in typical optimistic fashion:

"We hope that the home will be such a success that we will be compelled to enlarge it in a very short time. The whole thing is wonderfully sweet and beautiful to us, and we cannot realize our good fortune."

IV

A TRUE HEROINE

"I call her a true heroine. She literally gave her life; not in one furious crisis but every day for 43 years and more."*

Miss Florence claims, with a twinkle in her eyes, that the first resident of the home for blind women was a man. Actually a blind broommaker was among the first. The man had come to the Traders for help, and they had sent him to Columbus to learn a trade. Released from the school as a broommaker, he had no place to ply his trade. So the girls set him up first in the barn at Clovernook, later moved him into a three-room cottage which had been built on the place. Although Mr. Procter had said he would buy Clovernook, but not support it, his generous hand is detected in the early history of the home, until the time of his death. It was he who built the cottage, for the broommaker and a gardener.

The first three women residents moved into the home the Monday after its dedication. In a short time the family numbered 10, crowded into the little eight-room house, with no city water, no gas and no electricity. By 1912, 13 women were living there.

"When all of the inmates are seated in the tiny dining room, neither door can be opened," is the way a writer of the time pictured the set-up.

The going wasn't easy for Clovernook's trustees. At

*Canon Gilbert Symons

first, when income failed to cover expenses, Georgia and Florence had to raid the countryside for help. Once, when supplies fell short, they decided to invade the nearby city of Hamilton. Armed with a letter of introduction to one prominent citizen, they were passed down the line to others, and came back that evening with $250 in cash and checks. One business man of the period confided that he always was moved to dig into his pockets because of the "youth, beauty, lovely manners and splendid courage" of the women. Another told a friend of the Traders:

"You can't resist the appeal of those earnest, sweet-faced petitioners."

Helen Keller, with whom the girls had several rewarding contacts, once said: "The heaviest burden on the blind is not blindness, but idleness."

George Trader said: "Blindness and idleness are not to be endured."

From the moment Clovernook opened, the two sisters were as concerned with the mental welfare of its residents as they were with their physical care. The home soon became widely known as an industrial home for the blind.

Not long after they had their first grateful charges bedded down in the Cary cottage, Georgia and Florence journeyed to Lebanon, Ohio, to visit a weaving operation in a Quaker village. Shortly after their return to Cincinnati, several large weaving looms arrived at Clovernook—a donation from the Quakers.

The looms were set up in the barn, and soon rugs, coverlets and the like were coming from them. Blind women not strong enough to handle the looms were kept busy knitting, crocheting and doing bead work. The bead work was soon discarded by Georgia.

"People only buy it for charity, and that idea is what we want to eliminate from the minds of the blind," she declared.

When the first loom began to spin its colorful yarns, the Trader girls initiated a practice that has continued throughout all of Clovernook's busy, industrial career. The blind workers are paid a small salary for their work. With the money, they can buy their own clothes and enjoy some feeling of independence.

In 1910, the gift of a printing press by Mrs. Jennie March inaugurated the industrial project that was to make Clovernook known throughout the world. Equipped to print in the New York Point system, it was the first press ever operated for the blind in Cincinnati. By 1922, Clovernook's printing operation was the second largest printing house of books for the blind in the United States, the first being a house run by the government in Louisville. As late as 1931, Clovernook had one of only four presses in this country equipped to print Braille books, and it was the only one of the four operated by the blind. The Braille system had been adopted in 1920 as the universal system for printing for the blind.

In 1931, when the United States Government appropriated $100,000 for the printing of Braille books, Clovernook entered its bid. Back came an order for six books, specifying from 30 to 60 copies of each book.

V

CLOVERNOOK'S FRIENDS

*"We thank Thee for her large circle of friends in all walks of life."**

A local business man recently wagered that the Trader girls could have headed up a Community Chest drive, and come through with flying colors. Their story never would have unfolded to such shining heights had they not possessed a unique talent for enlisting support from all economic levels.

Not long ago Miss Florence entered a Cincinnati hospital for a check-up. A routine question still brings a smile to her lovely face. Had she, her examiner asked, ever done any hard labor?

"My sister and I labored real hard to raise money," was her quiet reply.

Income for Clovernook's expansion and operation has come roughly from three separate overall sources. One is donations, large and small, through special appeals. Another is the sale of products made by the blind; annual fetes, and other money-making projects. The third is bequests. All of the money, according to the best business heads, has been used wisely.

William A. Procter's name heads the list of Cincinnatians, prominent in the social and cultural life of the city, who gave generously from their fortunes to advance the work of the Trader girls.

*The Rev. Dr. G. Barrett Rich

Clovernook's now large plant, both working and resident, could be dissected over a span of 50 years, with name tags, many and few, attached to each unit.

Two prominent Cincinnatians, Mrs. Thomas J. Emery and Professor Philip Van Ness Myers, contributed $1,000 each to build the first main working quarters, a weaving shop constructed in 1907. Mrs. Emery had worked with and assisted the Traders financially since the early days of the library. Professor Myers, hailed at his death as one of the world's great historians, brought city water and gas to Clovernook in 1910 and electricity in 1914. In his will, he asked his widow to make a bequest in her will of $10,000 to Clovernook.

In 1913, an addition to the weaving shop provided headquarters for the printing operation. Subsequent additions, through the year 1941, have produced a sprawling, two-story panorama of connecting white frame buildings. Today they house the printing and weaving operations and an office.

The little Cary cottage is now dwarfed by the main living quarters of Clovernook. Georgia's prediction that success of the home would compel them to enlarge its quarters bore fruit in 1913. At the home's tenth anniversary, a new $15,000 building was opened. It was of rough red brick, in colonial style, with bedrooms, living room, dining room, kitchen and office, and large upper and lower porches on the southern exposure. Money for the building has been obtained through public subscription, begun with a $1,000 donation from Peter G. Thomson.

In 1920, Mr. Thomson's generosity added a four-bed hospital. In 1926, Clovernook's biggest building project was completed. It was a $50,000 addition to the main building, again accomplished through public subscription. Connected with the original structure by a solarium on each of three floors, it had underneath it a gymnasium.

Again familiar names headed the list of contributors: Mr. Thomson, Professor Myers, Mrs. Emery and William A. Procter's son, William Cooper Procter.

In 1930, a gift of $25,000 from Miss F. H. Rawson made possible enlarging of the printing shop and dining room. Bit by bit, in single and large doses, friends of the blind and of the Misses Trader have built Clovernook to its present wonderful state. For years Mr. Thomson, who was head of the Champion Coated Paper Company, gave quantities of paper to the printing shop—in 1930 alone it amounted to 7,749 pounds. John Omwake, president of the United States Playing Card Company, began in the early days to donate the playing cards for marking. That practice is continued to this day.

The annual fetes at the home had three principal goals. They raised funds. They supplied another outlet for articles made by the blind. They brought people to the home to see its good work.

The fetes were gay, colorful events. Heralded and promoted in advance in the local papers, they had their biggest coverage in the Cincinnati Enquirer's society pages. That newspaper's society editor for many years, Marion Devereux, would fill six columns of space before, and two or three more afterward. Widely known for her fancy and exultant prose, her long sentences and endless paragraphs, she displayed the best of her talents in pleading editorially for aid to the blind.

Society women, young and old, strung Japanese lanterns throughout the lawns, donned elaborate costumes and manned endless booths. A monologist would be a Taft or a Rawson, a Procter or a Resor. One of the Misses Worthington would be telling fortunes, while a Thomson, Pogue or Shillito was reading palms. Neaves, Gholsons, Crabbs and Warringtons strolled the grounds as gypsy singers or staged little dramas, rehearsed for weeks in advance.

Often nearby Ohio Military Institute sent over its boys' brass band; several times, the Ft. Thomas Military Band was there in force, 25-strong, with brass, bugle and kettledrum. Inside the Cary cottage, afternoon tea always was served, with two young debutantes impersonating the poet sisters.

The first fete was at Clovernook's opening in 1903. None have been held since Georgia's death. The home's 50th anniversary, in 1953, was observed with a brief program, followed by tea.

No fete was given in 1916, because of the illness of both Mr. and Mrs. Trader. Mr. Trader died in 1918. Plans were abandoned for the fete in 1921, when Mrs. Trader died.

In 1919, a newspaper clipping tells of arrangements for that year's fete, the first in two years because of World War I. Clovernook's coffers, it was reported, "threaten to collapse, so greatly have they shrunk since 1917."

Three other years in the long span saw no fetes at Clovernook; in 1929 because of remodeling of the workshop and other buildings; in 1930 because Georgia and Florence, following a siege of the grippe, had not returned from Florida in time, and in 1937, because Hamilton Pike was being repaved.

Sales of articles made by Clovernook residents were not confined to the fetes. Week-long bazaars, presided over by volunteers, were conducted at Cincinnati's Burnet and Gibson Houses and St. Nicholas Hotel. Special money-making projects also commanded the attention of society at intervals. David Bispham, a famous baritone of the day, was presented in a benefit recital in 1905 at the Grand Opera House. In 1914, a "Cafe Chantant" at the Hotel Sinton was so big and glamorous that one society reporter was moved to write:

"Had sweet Alice Cary been among the merry gathering at the Sinton last night, she would have had another 'beautiful picture to hang on memory's wall.' "

Public sentiment for Clovernook caught on quickly. In December, 1903, just six months after the tiny home for the blind opened, the Commercial Tribune conducted a coupon contest to decide the "most popular charitable institution in the city." First prize—$500 worth of groceries from the Kroger Grocery and Baking Company.

All the Traders and their friends got on the telephone and wrote letters to their friends. Clovernook won, hands down.

Bequests to Clovernook, ranging from $10,000 to $40,000, were, and still are, not uncommon. Added to regular donations, in units of from $1 to $100, and countless gifts in memoriam, they total quite a sum. When operating expenses were paid, Georgia and Florence asked their advisors to invest the balance.

Clovernook is in good shape today; such good shape that it operates with the hearty approval of Cincinnati's Community Chest, but with no financial help from the Chest. Only the continued aid of its friends keeps it in that healthy condition.

VI

LIFE ON TIPTOES

"For those who knew you, dread of age is past!
You who took life, tiptoe, to the very last;
It never lost for you its lovely look
You kept your interest in its thrilling book."*

The devotion of all four of the Trader sisters was a rare and beautiful thing.

Effie, the eldest, was an artist of more than local prominence; often her fine hand was found in the colorful decorations at Clovernook fetes, and in the plans for its various buildings.

Louise Trader was "the baby" of the family, adored by them all. She loved to sing, and possessed a sweet and pleasing voice. Of the four sisters, Louise was considered the merriest and most even tempered.

From early childhood, Florence had woven her own life into that of her blind sister; they soon became one in sight and spirit. As the two women walked together, briskly and with no hesitation, the sighted sister's hand would be tucked through the arm of the blind one. Every turn or pressure of Florence's hand meant something; a step up or down, a turn to right or left.

Although more frail than robust, Florence was the Trojan of the quartet. On the long motor trips taken by the sisters, she was always at the wheel. Florence took the major role in packing and unpacking; delivered pic-

*Roselle M. Montgomery

GEORGIA
DUCKWORTH
TRADER

FLORENCE
BISHOP
TRADER

EFFIE CORWIN TRADER

LOUISE KING TRADER

tures to Effie's patrons, watched over Louise's health and welfare, and spent the rest of her time working with, and adoring, "Georgie."

The blind sister had a magnetic personality that drew everyone to her. A dainty and fragile looking woman, she had a crown of soft brown hair, and delicate features. Georgia had a sympathetic way with people, which probably made her the good teacher that she was. Kindly and courteous, as were all the sisters, she was always ready to listen.

Her untiring interest in helping others similarly afflicted, in the face of her fragility, touched the hearts and admiration of the stoutest of men. In 1928, when the Cincinnati Lions Club adopted a new lioness at the local Zoo, they asked for and received permission to name her "Georgia."

Murray Seasongood, after her death, pictured Georgia as 'buoyant, idealistic, practical, imaginative, and generous."

"Although blind", her old schoolmate continued, "she had many compensating blessings, which lighted up her vale of darkness: the devotion of her sisters, a keen, selfless and, when occasion required, a businesslike mind . . . "

In the early part of the century, Georgia and Florence took several winter vacations in Florida, sent there apparently by parents and friends to get them away from their endless ministrations to others. Their letters from there to William A. Procter, lonely and aging, following the death of his wife, were by his own admission "read and re-read." One of his to them, the winter of 1905, had this admonition:

"Now I want Florence, as well as Georgia, to relax. If you don't you may have to stay all summer!"

By 1913, when they bought their first automobile, all four girls were taking motor trips together. In 1921, Florence started to keep a diary of their travels. Ordinarily their destination was Florida in the winter, Massachusetts in the summer.

Their days were full, and followed a schedule typical of gentlewomen of the period. Sightseeing; driving; shopping; calling; being called upon; meeting friends for luncheon, tea or dinner; playing bridge; visiting antique shops; going to the theater; writing letters, reading and resting in all their pleasant details, fill pages of Florence's diaries. Interspersed were hours spent by Effie painting, and visits to institutions for the blind, wherever they could find them.

Their friends were legion. Farewell parties preceded their departure, and floral tributes welcomed them home. In 1928, when the four sisters went to Europe for the summer, Florence sat down in her stateroom on the SS Providence and recorded receipt of: 40 letters, nine telegrams; 32 pounds of candy and nuts; five books; four large boxes of flowers, and two huge baskets of fruit.

Later, in a Paris hotel, this typical entry was made: "Georgia and I have balcony, where we can sit and see the Tuilleries Gardens on the Rue de Rivoli."

Sightseeing, on foot or on burrows, as they did in the Spanish countryside, always found Georgia in the group. She loved nothing better than to accompany her sisters to Europe's old churches and museums, where she could "feel" the beauty.

In 1944, about 8 o'clock in the morning, the mortal bond among the four sisters was first broken. Georgia had a heart attack, and died. That same year Effie had a heart attack, but two years later the three sisters were in Rockport, Massachusetts, for the summer, and Effie had started to paint again. In 1951, a short time after winning first prize for the best oil in an exhibition at the Corcoran Gallery in Washington, Effie died.

Several years previously, the house on Hale Avenue

had been sold, and another bought at 3000 Vernon Place, also in Avondale. Not long after Effie's passing, Florence and Louise sold the second house, and moved into a roomy, old-fashioned four-room apartment. While they set off once again for Rockport, an artist friend hung 45 of Effie's paintings on the walls of the apartment.

Life, surrounded by Effie's pictures and mementos of Georgia's good works, goes on pretty much the same for the two remaining sisters. Plans for a trip to Europe early in 1957 were abandoned in favor of a cruise to Hawaii, where there was no war scare.

Asked why her diaries have no entries about their life in Cincinnati, Florence answered quickly:

"I knew what we were doing when we were at home."

Florence still knows, without any reminding notations. As sole trustee of Clovernook and secretary-treasurer of the Cincinnati Library Society for the Blind, she is carrying on her blind sister's interest in life's "thrilling book."

VII

TWO ANGELS

"Sometimes when I look at those two girls, I wonder if Florence isn't almost as much of an angel as Georgie?"

William A. Procter was quoted by one of his daughters as having said this often. In one form or another, the phrase has been echoed many times by admirers of the two Trader sisters.

Both Georgia and Florence received many honors. Cincinnati's Academy of Medicine and Ophthalmological Association, in 1927, staged a dinner around them at the local University Club. It was "to give public recognition of the immeasurable service given to the blind not only of Cincinnati but, from impetus here, to the entire country."

The biggest single honor accorded the two sisters, on June 15, 1944, had to be accepted by Florence alone. To her, and to Georgia posthumously, went the Migel Medal for outstanding service to the blind.

The medal was bestowed by the American Foundation for the Blind, of which M. C. Migel was president. Honored with the Trader sisters was Henry Ford, who also received a medal for his company's pioneer work in finding satisfactory employment for the handicapped. At the presentation ceremony in New York, Henry Ford II shared the spotlight with Florence, as he accepted the medal for his grandfather.

It was but three short months after Georgia's death

that word came from New York of the honor, with an invitation to attend the ceremony. Heartbroken over the loss of her sister, Florence felt that she could not go through with it. Again and again, encouraged by her friends, she tried to write an acceptance speech.

Finally, without the speech, she and Effie and Louise left for New York. No reporter took down that important day what words came from Florence's heart. But the text of the presentation speech, made by Helen Keller, has been preserved. It said, in part:

"What touches me especially is the wonderful companionship that united you two women during a lifetime of constructive intelligence and amazingly many-sided service to the blind of Cincinnati."

"Each transmuting the other's generous dreams into deeds of ministering love, you have had a foretaste of Heaven's communion, as well as a glorious increase in power of accomplishment.

"The true greatness of your work is not merely in the enterprises you undertook. It is in the genius for friendship and encouragement with which you have achieved them all."

These words, from a fellow angel of the blind, are part of the wonderful heritage left by Georgia to her sister. As for Florence, she is still transmuting the generous dreams that she and her blind sister shared, into deeds of ministering love.

VIII

A PATH OF ROSES

*"They strewed life's path with roses,
as they wandered up and down."**

Over the years, the happiness and industry that prevailed at Clovernook were shared by other blind, both near and far. This again was due to the never-ceasing endeavors of the Trader sisters.

For many years, beginning shortly after the home was opened, annual picnics were given on the tree-shaded lawns. One would be for the adult blind of the city. The other was for blind children, the children that look downward.

Pinning the tail on the donkey was a favorite pastime of the sightless youngsters. They also loved the rides in the pony cart, and on the gentle Shetland pony. Many a child would wander among the flowers, or toward the barn, where the home's two cows, "Clover" and "Nook," were chewing their cuds.

A writer described one little boy, known among his sightless pals as an artist of vocal imitation. He spent the day following the birds, chickens and cows, in order to improve his imitations of their calls.

A few fortunate youngsters, three and four at a time, were brought from the hot city for summer vacations at Clovernook.

In 1919, the Trader sisters organized a campaign for

*Howard Saxby

gifts to the blind. Clovernook sent as Christmas greetings books in embossed type to soldiers blinded during the war. At that time, there were 1200 men so afflicted in St. Dunstan's, in England, and 100 in an institution in Baltimore. At a cost of only 25 cents per book, the blind girls at Clovernook were able to print, sew and bind the books.

It was in 1922 that a project for blind children was initiated at Clovernook by the Cincinnati Lions Club. In December of that year, a children's magazine was printed in Braille type and sent to blind children in Cincinnati and other Ohio cities. The following June, the Lions Club International voted at its convention to distribute the magazine throughout the United States and Canada. That wonderful work still is continued.

The donation of a radio to Clovernook, also in 1922, opened up new vistas for its residents. It was followed two years later by publishing of the "Braille Radio News," complete with dotted schedules.

Each year, Cincinnati's McDonald Printing Company donates the Traders' annual Clovernook report. Several of its pages are devoted to the friends of the blind who regularly give subscriptions to the radio news, and to Braille Christmas calendars, printed at Clovernook.

In 1934, the large library of books built up by the Library Society for the Blind was moved from the Public Library to Clovernook, where a second floor was added to the printing and weaving shops to accommodate it. Most of the books were being circulated in central and southern Ohio, and throughout Kentucky, Indiana and Tennessee. A nearby post office station at Mt. Healthy made it easy for trucks to pick up and deliver the books at Clovernook, twice a day.

Also in 1934, the Library of Congress began to supply "talking books" for the blind throughout the country. Talking books are recorded readings of literature and other writings. Clovernook's library got its share of the books, and a goodly number of subscribers also. One talking book, of "Gone with the Wind," came in four boxes, with 20 records in each box.

In December, 1955, the library was moved back downtown to the Public Library's annex at 617 College Street, right behind the Enquirer Building. The present quarters house a circulating library of more than 73,000 Braille and talking books for the blind. The library is administered by Miss Ethel Price, its librarian, and seven assistants.

Clovernook today conducts a healthy, busy printing plant. Eight million Braille pages are printed annually, and bound into books that are mailed and circulated free to the blind, in 27 regional libraries throughout the United States. Including the Lions magazine, a religious magazine, a magazine for teen-agers and one for blinded veterans, 84,000 such publications are printed yearly by Clovernook's blind women. In addition, there are the Braille calendars, the radio news and catalogs of books.

As for Clovernook's weaving department, 400 rugs are turned out there every month. The rugs and other handiwork are sold through department stores.

THE WORKSHOP, EMBRACING ALL THE ADDITIONS BUILT OVER THE YEARS

WEAVING DEPARTMENT

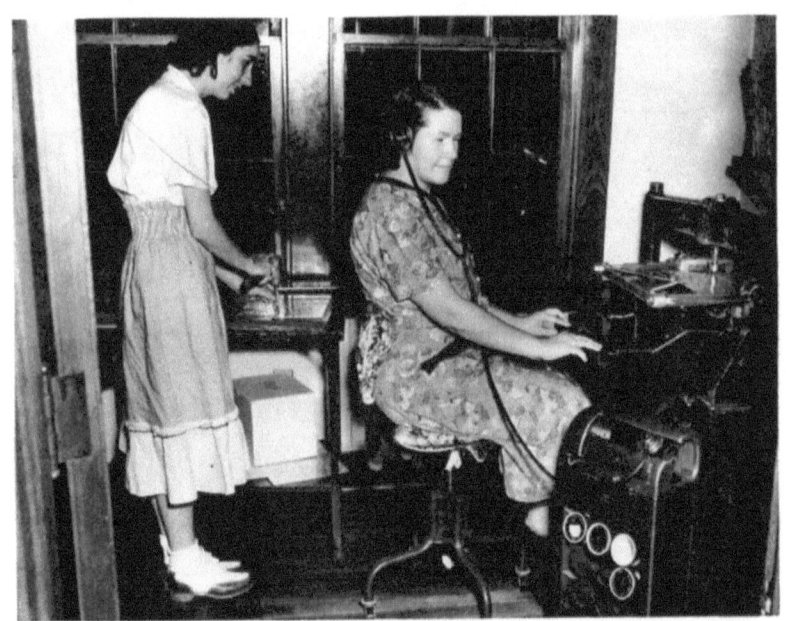
BLIND HERMINE HENDL TRANSCRIBES WORK ON ZINC PLATES

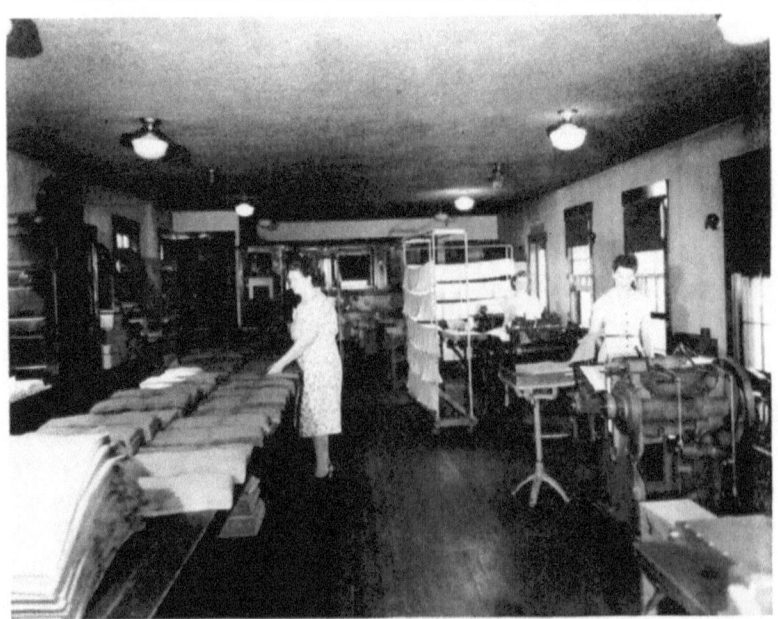
COLLATING THE BRAILLE PAGES

IX

THE DEAREST PLACE ON EARTH

> *"No words can ever express the gratitude I have for all the happiness I have had here ever since I entered the Home. To me, it is the dearest place on earth."**

Letters, by the bushelfuls, have brought much satisfaction to the Trader girls. Sometimes they come by local post from a Clovernook resident, moved by happiness to put her gratitude into written words. The others bear postmarks from all over the world.

"May God bless you all," is a typical ending. The writer may be sending a "thank you" for a book, a magazine, a calendar or a game.

On her frequent visits to Clovernook, Miss Florence glories in sitting down at a desk and reading the mail. A tear may come to her eyes, over a sentence here and there. But the quiet smile on her face spells a deep, almost religious feeling of satisfaction.

Miss Florence is the sole trustee of the home for the blind. A great source of help to her in carrying through her role is the three men who serve as her advisors. All three are descendants of two of Clovernook's earliest and largest benefactors. They are Samuel Benedict, a grandson of William A. Procter, and Dwight Johnston Thomson and Reuben A. Robertson, Jr., both grandsons of Peter Thomson.

Often Miss Florence takes a visitor with her to Clover-

*A Clovernook Resident

nook, driving her own car. With sure hands she swings into the driveway, past red brick sentinels that stand at either side of the entrance.

A hundred feet in, the car passes the Cary cottage, on the left, and the large red brick residence on the right. It stops to one side of the white frame workshop, close to where the old barn used to be.

Inside the shop, in a comfortable, bright office, sits the home's superintendent. She is Miss Anne M. Costello who, in February, 1957, celebrated her 41st anniversary as friend and adviser to the residents of the home.

A tour of the weaving and printing shops begins.

The minute Miss Florence walks into a room, a spell seems to be cast over the industry there. A touch of her hand on the shoulder of a blind worker brings an immediate smile of recognition. Conversation begins to pour out, with excited reports of progress being made.

Mabel Knox is at one of the Quaker looms, turning out one of those multi-colored "Hit and Miss" rugs. She has called Clovernook "home" for nine years. Nearby is Rosanne Masters, a veteran of 33 years. Her assignment today is blanket weaving. Quickly she explains that she also works in the print shop, and crochets rugs in the evenings.

The visitor is then guided down the web of hallways, brought about by the workshop's many additions, and shown the amazing printing operation. It is divided over a series of small and large rooms. In the smaller ones, manuscripts are recorded into dictaphones by sighted workers; transcriptions are made on a stereotype machine, and proof reading and corrections go on. The press and binding operations are in the larger rooms.

The entire process of Braille printing is a fascinating thing to behold. Braille employs a system of raised dots on paper, which are interpreted by the fingers of the blind.

The letters of the alphabet are formed by various combinations of a basic six dots, placed in different positions.

Blind Hermine Hendl, who is known around Clovernook as a "wonderful stereotyper," was at work in the first step in Braille printing. Seated at a machine, earphones fitted to her head, she was transcribing words onto a rectangular zinc plate, about the size of a big geography book. As she listened to the words, her fingers with lightning-like speed and efficiency punched appropriate keys on the machine. Small steel bars leaped up, under electric propulsion, and punched closed holes, signifying the letters, into the zinc plate.

Hermine's manuscript was from the textbook "How to Write and Sell Fiction." The book, she explained, would run over 200 pages embossed, through a recent improvement in Braille stereotyping, on both sides of the plate. Hermine then displayed a rare accomplishment for a blind worker. She is able to make her own corrections on a plate, done with a hammer and hand punch. The false indentations are punched flat.

The finished plates go to a power press, operated by sighted women, where the first sheet to come off the press is a proof sheet. On the press, dampened paper is sandwiched between the zinc plate and a sheet of rubber, and run through the revolving cylinder that constitutes the press. When the rubber is removed, the indentations in the zinc have produced corresponding indentations in the paper.

Claudine Johnson, who "loves the work" and has been at it for 18 years, was one of the blind readers to get the proof that day. Seated in a small room, she was reading the proof aloud, while a sighted helper checked the ink manuscript. In another room, Josephine Matthews, with 13 years of experience behind her, was trying to find more mistakes. Often, a blind worker will walk down the hall to consult a big Braille dictionary.

The finished plates are then put on regular presses, and the actual printing of the Braille begun. When all the pages are assembled and sorted, they are passed on to the binding department. There the giant volumes are sewn together, covered and titled, all by blind workers. The hand stitching, an almost lost art in the publishing business today, is a delight to watch.

The tour ends in a little exhibition room, where samples of the books and magazines are on display. A Braille copy of "Booker T. Washington," a biography by Basil Matthews, is an interesting example. The regularly printed edition of the book covers 337 pages, the Braille version 591 pages. The Braille embraces four volumes, each two and three-quarter inches thick. The pages are ten and one half inches in width, eleven and one quarter inches in length.

In this room also, records are kept for Clovernook's vast mailing operation of magazines. The boxes of addressoplates contain 259 foreign names, including 52 in England, 102 in the Philippines and 78 in Canada.

The blind women work seven hours a day, five days a week. At lunch time, they leave their presses and their looms and walk securely to the big red brick residence, along a cement sidewalk. All the walks at Clovernook are lined with iron guide rails.

The residence building faces west on Hamilton Avenue. A walk into the entrance hall gives the visitor an immediate feeling of a private home. For obvious reasons, there are no rugs or carpeting on the floors. But comfortable furniture, including a grand piano, is found in a large living room to the right. Brightening all the walls of the downstairs rooms are many of Effie Trader's paintings.

The dining room, at the left of the hall, is ready for luncheon. Soon the women are seated at long, narrow tables, set up with pretty dishes and table linen.

After luncheon, an automatic elevator, installed in 1950, lifts Miss Florence and her visitors to the second and third floors. The rooms on these floors include 37 comfortable bedrooms which have taken on the individuality of each occupant. All have radios. Many have on their dressers pictures of loved ones, which never have been seen by their owners.

A sudden thought envelops the visitor.

Georgia Trader never saw Clovernook and its lovely acres either, in a physical sense. The whole picture, for her, was but a fine etching in her private museum of love and beauty.

The solariums, which in 1926 served to connect the annex to the main building, are verdant with plants, owned and tended by the blind women. Each also contains a television set. The sets boast burned-out picture tubes, but have healthy sound apparatus. They are for favorite programs, which are not carried on radio.

A visit to the Cary cottage is next on the tour. Its low-ceilinged rooms, with antique furniture of the period of the poet sisters, take the visitor back to thoughts of the early days of Clovernook. Over the fireplace in the living room is a portrait of William A. Procter. Over the piano are pictures of Alice and Phoebe Cary.

Guard rails also line the two closed-in stairways of the tiny cottage. One set of stairs, at the east end of the house, leads to two bedrooms; another set, on the west, to two more. Underneath the front stairs is the nostalgic manuscript cupboard of the poet sisters.

Miss Florence and her visitor close the cottage door behind them. Looking out over Clovernook's blessed acres, and the satisfaction inherent in them, the lines of Phoebe Cary's hymn come to mind:

> *"One sweetly solemn thought*
> *Comes to me o'er and o'er*
> *I'm nearer home today, today*
> *Than I have been before."*

www.ingramcontent.com/pod-product-compliance
Lightning Source LLC
Chambersburg PA
CBHW030140100526
44592CB00011B/980